Draw with ART FOR KIDS HUB

DINOSAURS

30 step-by-step drawing projects inside!

Rob Jensen

Senior Designer Emma Wicks
Senior Production Editor Jennifer Murray
Senior Production Controller Louise Minihane
Senior Acquisitions Editor Pete Jorgensen
Managing Art Editor Jo Connor
Managing Director Mark Searle
Written and Illustrated by Rob Jensen

Designed and Edited by Elizabeth T. Gilbert and Rebecca Razo
at Coffee Cup Creative, LLC.

Copyedited by Beth Adelman

First American Edition, 2025
Published in the United States by DK Publishing
1745 Broadway, 20th Floor, New York, NY 10019

25 26 27 28 29 10 9 8 7 6 5 4 3 2 1
001-350735-Oct/2025

A catalog record for this book
is available from the Library of Congress.
ISBN 978-0-5939-7049-2

DK books are available at special discounts when purchased in bulk for sales promotions, premiums, fund-raising, or educational use.
For details, contact: DK Publishing Special Markets,
1745 Broadway, 20th Floor, New York, NY 10019
SpecialSales@dk.com

Printed and bound in China

www.dk.com

www.artforkidshub.com

This book was made with Forest Stewardship Council™ certified paper – one small step in DK's commitment to a sustainable future.
Learn more at www.dk.com/uk/information/sustainability

Draw with Art for Kids Hub

DINOSAURS

30 step-by-step drawing projects inside!

Rob Jensen

Table of CONTENTS

Welcome to Art for Kids Hub!

Hey, fellow explorers!
I'm Rob. And along with my amazing wife, Teryn, and our four creative kids, Jack, Hadley, Austin, and Olivia, we make art together as a family—and we love sharing it with you! Dinosaurs are fascinating creatures, and we always have lots of fun exploring the prehistoric world through drawing.

This book is divided into two parts. In Part I, you'll find step-by-step drawing lessons for a variety of dino-themed projects. Each drawing is ranked Level 1, Level 2, or Level 3 according to its difficulty (see the Symbol Key on the opposite page). Don't worry, though! You'll be able to draw all the projects by following along step by step.

In Part II, you'll find tips for drawing backgrounds, props, and completed scenes. I've also included some RAWR-some folding surprise drawing projects at the very end. Whether you're a beginner or a budding artist, there's something fun for everyone.

Ready to begin? Grab your art tools and some paper, and let's make dinosaur art that brings smiles and creates joy!

ROB

TERYN

AUSTIN

JACK

OLIVIA

HADLEY

About This Book

For each project, follow the steps in red to complete your drawing. Then add color using your favorite art tools. It's as simple as that!

Symbol Key

Each project is marked with one of the following symbols, from less difficult to a little more challenging. But don't be afraid to try them all!

 = Level 1

 = Level 2

 = Level 3

 = Great work!

MORE IN THIS BOOK

- ☑ Draw a volcano, fossils, insects, prehistoric trees, and other dino-themed props.
- ☑ Combine drawings to make completed scenes.
- ☑ Create fun folding surprise drawings.

Art Tools & SUPPLIES

Here are some art tools you can use to draw and color the projects in this book. These are some of my favorite supplies, but you can use any tools that are available to you.

Black Marker

I like to draw with a permanent black marker for a bold, solid outline. But feel free to begin your drawings with pencil if you prefer.

Paper

White marker paper is perfect if you're using markers to color, and regular paper is fine if you're using crayons or colored pencils.

CHECKLIST

- [x] A flat drawing surface, like a table or clipboard
- [x] Marker paper
- [x] Black permanent marker
- [x] Pencil and sharpener
- [x] Coloring tools, such as colored pencils, markers, and crayons

Markers

Markers create smooth, solid strokes of color. Some sets include both fine tips and thick tips. I use alcohol-based markers because they dry quickly, and their colors don't fade easily.

Crayons

Wax crayons are inexpensive and easy to find. Sometimes they create a bumpy texture and can be hard to blend, so I use gel crayons. They are creamy and extra smooth.

Colored Pencils

These tools are clean and simple. You can even layer them to blend and shade. Keep a sharpener on hand for pointy tips.

Pastels

There are two types of pastels: soft pastels and oil pastels. Soft pastels feel like chalk and create smooth, light blends. Oil pastels feel more like crayons and create bold, bright strokes.

We would LOVE to see your drawings! Learn how to share them with us here.

Brushes

Brushes come in a range of sizes and shapes. Brushes with natural bristles are best for watercolor paints, and synthetic bristles are best for acrylics. When you've finished painting, rinse your brushes with soap and warm water, and reshape the bristles before they dry.

Paints

Watercolor, tempera, and acrylic are water-based paints that you can use to color your art. Be sure to use them on sturdy paper, such as watercolor paper. While you paint, keep a cup of water nearby for rinsing your brushes—and have plenty of paper towels on hand for cleanup.

WATERCOLOR

TEMPERA

ACRYLIC

What Are DINOSAURS?

The word *dinosaur* means "terrible lizard" in Greek.

Before you start drawing, it helps to know a little bit about the subject. Dinosaurs are a group of extinct reptiles that roamed the Earth millions of years ago during the Mesozoic Era. They lived alongside other prehistoric creatures, such as flying reptiles (like the Pterodactyl, page 62) and marine reptiles (like the Plesiosaurus, page 70). Everything we know about the dinosaurs and prehistoric animals comes from the geologic record, which tells the story of Earth preserved within layers of rock. Fossils of teeth, bones, footprints, and more found in rock provide clues to how these animals looked, moved, and behaved.

66 MILLION YEARS AGO

252 MILLION YEARS AGO

Mesozoic Era

The Mesozoic Era, also called the "Age of the Dinosaurs," began about 252 million years ago and ended about 66 million years ago. During this era, reptiles dominated the Earth over land, sky, and sea. The Mesozoic Era is divided into the Triassic, Jurassic, and Cretaceous Periods. Be on the lookout for signs (shown below) that tell you the period when each dinosaur first appeared. Some dinosaurs existed over more than one time period.

TRIASSIC PERIOD

• 252–201 million years ago •

At the beginning of the Triassic Period, Earth's land was one large mass called Pangaea. Small, lightweight dinosaurs and marine-dwelling reptiles first appeared during this period.

TRIASSIC

JURASSIC PERIOD

• 201–145 million years ago •

During this period, Pangaea began to separate, forming the continents. Earth was warm and humid with shallow seas and forests, making way for birds and giant plant-eating dinosaurs called sauropods.

CRETACEOUS PERIOD

• 145–66 million years ago •

Flowering plants emerged and top predators (such as T. rex) dominated the land. Scientists believe a large asteroid hit Earth, leading to the end of the Cretaceous Period and the extinction of dinosaurs.

Getting STARTED

Before you begin drawing, it's a great idea to warm up. From dots and swirls to dashes and curls, make all sorts of marks on scrap paper to get the creative juices flowing.

I use a lot of loops, dots, and curvy, squiggly, and jagged lines in my drawings. What other lines and scribbles can you make?

Basic Shapes

Most of the drawings in the book incorporate familiar shapes like circles, triangles, squares, and ovals. Practice drawing these basic shapes and then draw new shapes of your own, if you like.

TRIANGLES

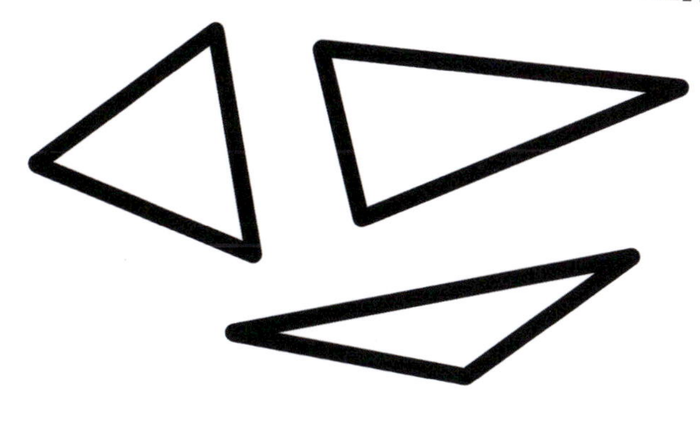

CIRCLES, OVALS & BEAN SHAPES

SQUARES, RECTANGLES & DIAMONDS

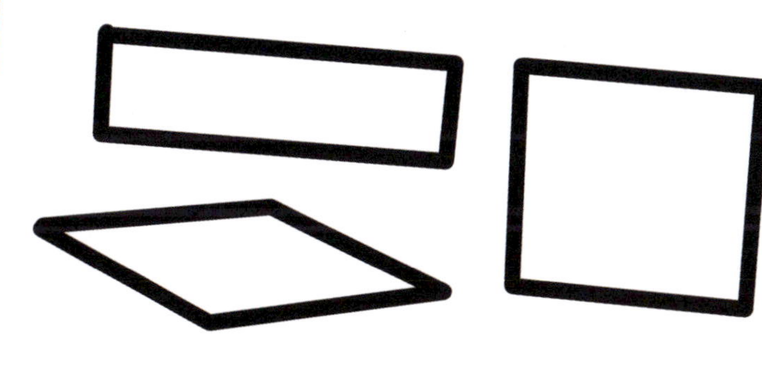

All About COLOR

The Color Wheel

The color wheel is a visual aid for understanding how colors work together. The colors on this wheel are divided into two groups: primary (blue, yellow, red) and secondary (green, orange, purple).

Complementary Colors

Complementary colors are two colors that are opposite each other on the color wheel. When they're placed next to each other in a drawing or painting, they appear brighter. Some examples are yellow and purple, blue and orange, and red and green.

Color Temperature

Colors are divided into two temperatures: cool and warm. Blue, green, and purple are cool colors. Yellow, orange, and red are warm colors. Color temperature plays a part in the mood of a drawing. For example, cool colors are calm and warm colors are energetic.

Color Mixing

Every color combination begins with the primary colors. Secondary colors are made by mixing two primary colors. Yellow + red = orange, red + blue = purple, and blue + yellow = green. Gray is made by mixing white and black, while pink is made from a combination of white and red. White lightens colors; black darkens colors.

Coloring Steps

To bring your characters to life, try this three-step approach to adding color.

Add smooth, flat areas of color with your tools of choice.

Layer your colors—or use slightly darker shades—to create shadows.

Finish coloring your art by adding highlights with white.

I like to get creative with color in my drawings! How about you?

Part 1: STEP-BY-STEP PROJECTS

Hey, art friends!

We love learning about and drawing dinosaurs! To draw the creatures in this section, start with step 1 and continue to follow each new step in red. Along the way, you'll find lots of encouragement, helpful art tips, and even some fun and interesting facts.

I had so much fun creating these drawing lessons, but we especially love drawing together as a family. So, in addition to my drawings, you'll also see tons of great drawings by Teryn, Jack, Hadley, Austin, and Olivia. Each of us has our own art style, and we want to inspire you to draw in your own unique style, too. There are no mistakes and no wrong ways to make art—the important thing is to have fun and practice!

Happy creating!

Pip & Polly the PALEONTOLOGISTS

I gave my paleontologist lots of pockets and a shovel for digging up fossils.

Want to add bones or fossils to your paleontologist scene? Turn to page 82 for ideas!

Begin by drawing the heads, faces, and brims of the hats.

1

2

3

Follow the steps in red to finish the heads and bodies.

4

5

6

Draw the legs, feet, and arms. Add pockets and the other details.

7

8

Complete the characters and add a shovel or other tools.

9

DID YOU KNOW?

Mary Anning was a pioneer in the field of paleontology. Born in England in 1799, she became a self-taught fossil hunter and made important discoveries from the Jurassic Period. She was the first explorer to uncover a nearly complete Plesiosaurus skeleton (page 70).

Benny the BRACHIOSAURUS

Begin with the eye and face. Then draw the mouth, the front of the neck, and a front leg.

1

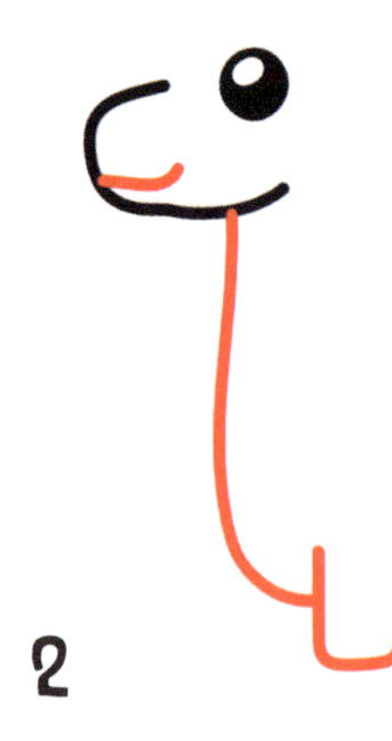

2

Finish the head and neck. Then add legs and the underside of the tail.

3

4

Use a curved line for the back and tail. Then add upside-down U shapes for toenails.

5

Draw a Brachiosaurus family and distinguish each member by the length of its neck. A dad Brachiosaurus might have the longest neck in the group, while a baby might have the shortest.

DID YOU KNOW?

Like the giraffe, the Brachiosaurus had longer front legs than back legs. This, along with its long neck, allowed it to reach and eat leaves high up in the trees.

1

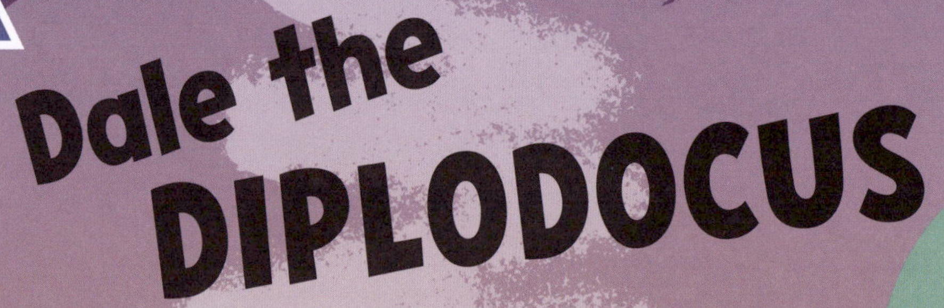

Dale the DIPLODOCUS

DID YOU KNOW?

As one of the longest dinosaurs discovered, the Diplodocus stretched about 80 feet from its head to the tip of its tail. Its tail alone contained 80 bones.

I added scales to my dino, but you can color yours in stripes, dots, or even swirls.

JURASSIC

I colored my dino purple and orange, which are secondary colors. Turn to page 14 to review color combinations.

Draw the eye and mouth. Then add the top of the head, neck, and front leg.

1

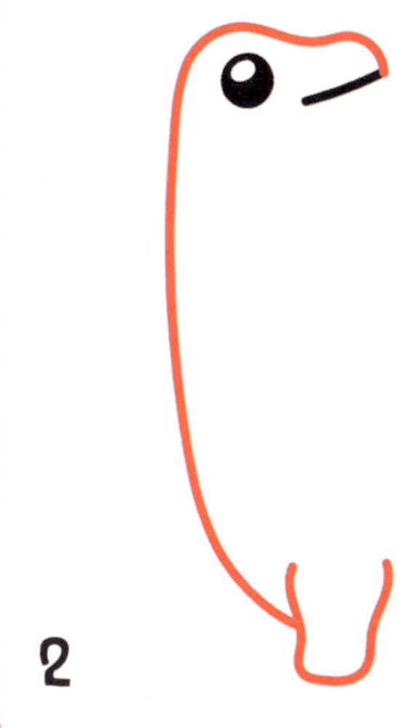

2

Now add the nostril, jaw, legs, and long, swooshing tail.

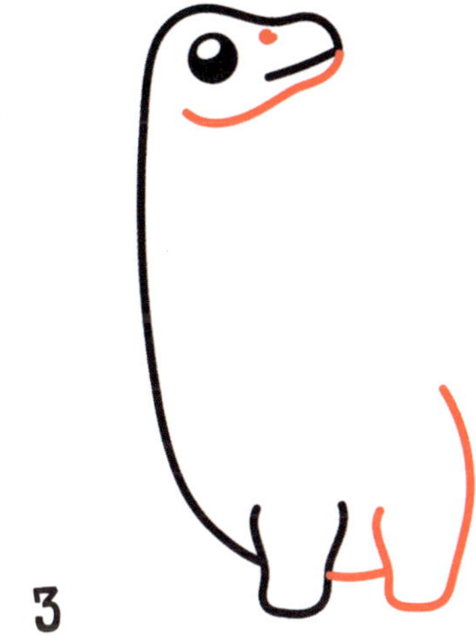

3

4

Draw a long line to complete the neck, back, and tail. Finish by adding toenails.

5

1

Pete the PARASAUROLOPHUS

Draw the eye and front of the head. Then add the flat, duck-billed mouth and nostrils.

1

2

Finish the crest and add the belly. Then draw the back of the head and start the limbs.

3

4

Add the swooping tail and back. Then finish the limbs and toenails.

5

6

Try This!

Scientists believe these dinos lived in herds. Draw a large gathering of Parasaurolophus roaming across a swampy landscape.

DID YOU KNOW?

This dinosaur is known for the distinct bony crest on its head. Scientists believe this creature used its crest to produce a low, horn-like sound to communicate with other dinosaurs of the same species.

CRETACEOUS
Hey Rob, what do you get when you cross a dinosaur with a firework?
Dino-mite!

2

Syd the STEGOSAURUS

Try This!

Feeling extra creative? Make each of your dino's plates a different color.

Begin by drawing the eye, head, and front of the body.

1

2

3

Add the front and hind legs, back, and tail. Then draw a triangular bony plate.

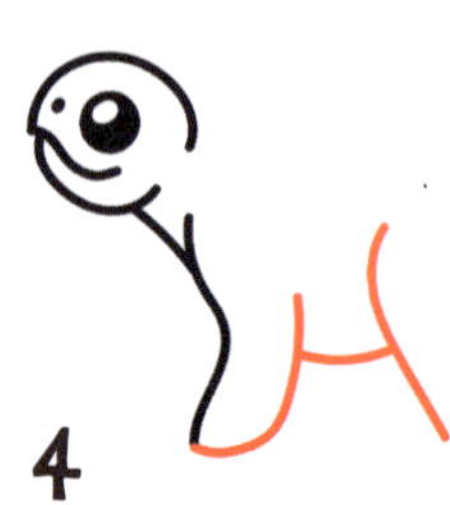

4

5

6

Draw more bony plates and spikes on the back and tail. Finish the legs and toenails.

7

8

DID YOU KNOW?
The Stegosaurus was an herbivore, or plant eater, with two rows of bony plates down its back. Sharp spikes at the end of the tail were likely used to defend itself against predators.
I outlined the yellow plates with red to add some dimension.
I made my Stegosaurus olive green with brown plates. I added a bit of yellow on its underside for contrast.
JURASSIC

3

Tina the TROODON

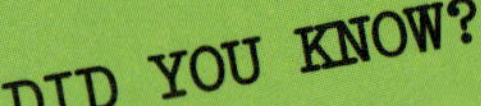

DID YOU KNOW?

Scientists believe that many dinosaurs, including the Troodon, were covered in feathers. In fact, birds are considered the closest living relatives of dinosaurs.

Experts don't know the exact colors of this dino's feathers, so have fun with your choices!

I used green and orange marker first. Then I added some darker colors for shading.

Try This!

Create an original dinosaur by mashing up two or more types into one! What would a Diplodocus (page 22), Stegosaurus (page 26), Troodon mashup look like?

Begin with a large eye and an open mouth. Then build the head and front of the body.

1

2

3

Add the rest of the limbs and body. Don't forget two rows of sharp teeth!

4

5

6

Add the tail, tongue, feathers, and other finishing details.

7

8

2

Ted the TRICERATOPS

Begin by drawing the beaked face. Add a triangular horn on the snout.

1

2

3

Complete the head and horns. Add the near side of the body.

4

5

6

Now add the frill, far limbs, and tail. Draw the curve of the back, and add skin folds and toenails.

7

8

Try This!

It's fun to imagine what Earth was like during the time of the dinosaurs. Turn to page 81 for some prop and scene ideas to incorporate into your drawings.

I

Cedric the COELOPHYSIS

DID YOU KNOW?

This quick, lightweight carnivore of the Late Triassic Period was about 10 feet long, 4 feet tall, and 50 pounds. It was one of the earliest dinosaurs to roam the Earth, existing about 150 million years before the famous T. rex (page 44).

Try This!

This dinosaur needs a sidekick. Draw a best friend to accompany Coelophysis on its adventures.

Draw the eye, mouth, face, head, and curved neck.

1

2

3

Begin drawing the four limbs, adding a line for the belly.

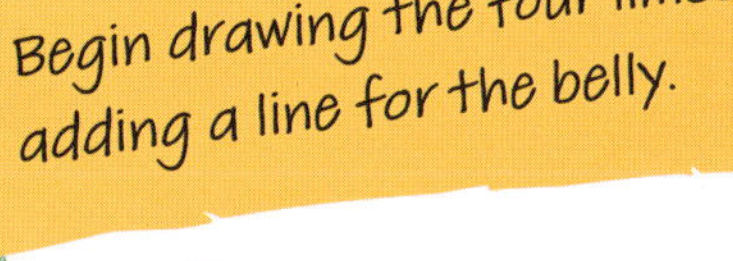

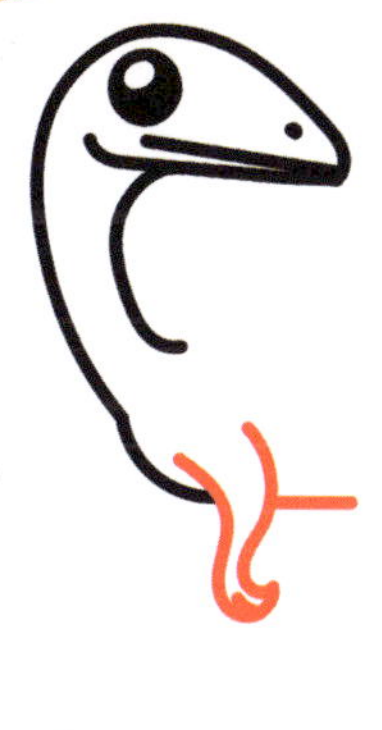

4

5

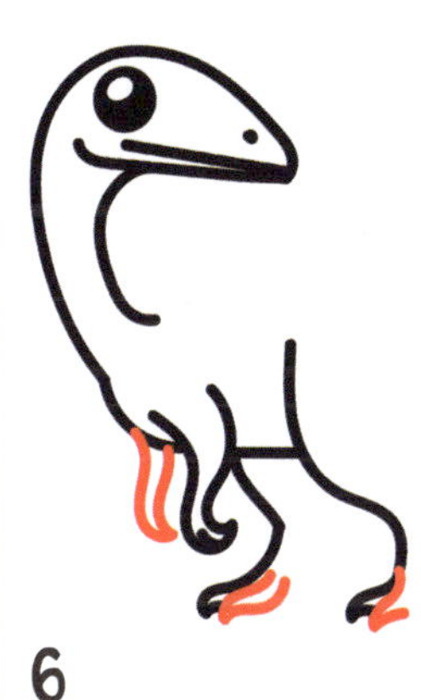

6

Complete the limbs and draw the tail and back. Add a few skin folds to finish.

7

8

2

Iggy the IGUANODON

Begin by drawing the eye, head, neck, and limbs. Don't forget the beak!

1

2

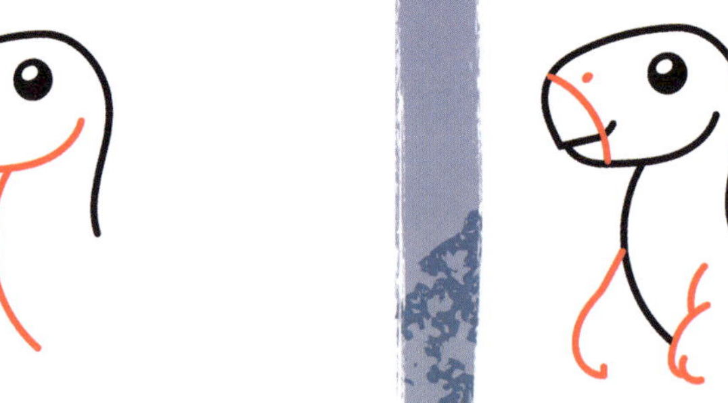

3

Follow the steps in red to build the limbs and body.

4

5

6

Now add the tail, wrinkles, toenails, and underbelly.

7

8

Try This!
This dinosaur roamed the Earth when flowering plants first appeared in the fossil record. It's a great reason to include lots of colorful flowers in your Iguanodon scenes!
The Iguanodon was a large herbivore with a toothless beak.
The Iguanodon also had a spike on each thumb, which it likely used for self-defense.
CRETACEOUS

Zach the THERIZINOSAURUS

Begin by drawing the eye and beaked face. Finish the head, and add the neck and claw.

1

2

3

Add the rest of the limbs, tail, and back. Use zigzags to show some feathering on the head and back.

4

5

6

To finish, add toenails, skin folds, and tail feathers.

7

DID YOU KNOW?

The fossils of this herbivore were discovered in what is now China and Mongolia. It's known for its very long claws, which it likely used to strip leaves and rake vegetation. Each claw was about 28 inches long!

Scott the CYMBOSPONDYLUS

I made mine green so it blends into the marine environment.

DID YOU KNOW?

This member of the Ichthyosaur family (page 48) was one of the first ocean giants. Cymbospondylus was about the size of a sperm whale, reaching 20 to 50 feet long!

Draw an arrow shape for the head and an eye. Add the mouth, nostril, and front of the neck.

Now, add the front fins, body, and tail.

Complete the details and add color.

Try This!

On a large piece of paper, draw an ocean for prehistoric marine life. Add a Plesiosaurus (page 70), a Henodus chelyops (page 74), and even a few sharks!

3

Annie the ARCHAEOPTERYX

DID YOU KNOW?

Archaeopteryx is a prehistoric flying creature that shared traits, including feathered wings, with modern birds. Like reptiles and dinosaurs, though, this creature had rows of teeth and a long, bony tail.

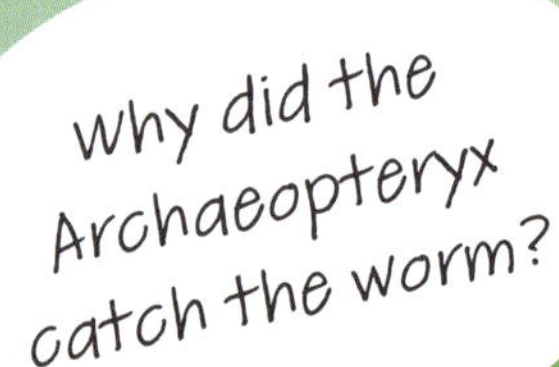

Why did the Archaeopteryx catch the worm?

Because it was an early bird!

Begin by drawing the face and feathered chest. Start the wing, using scooped strokes to suggest feathers.

1

2

3

Follow the steps in red to build the head, clawed wings, and feet.

4

5

6

Draw more wing feathers and add a fancy tail. Detail the feet.

7

8

3

Ally the ALLOSAURUS

JURASSIC

Start with the face, head, and neck. Draw tiny triangles for teeth.

1

2

3

Begin adding the limbs. Draw its sharp, curved claws.

4

5

6

Add a curved back and swooshing tail. Complete the limbs, and finish with toenails and skin folds.

7

8

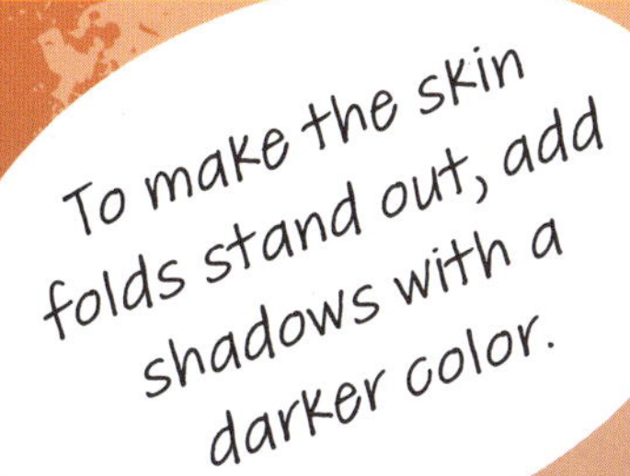

The Allosaurus has a bump above each eye, which may have provided protection from the sun.

Try This!

The Allosaurus lived in what is now North America. Are you interested in where each dinosaur was found? On a large sheet of paper, draw a world map, and add your dino drawings according to where they once roamed.

Ralph the TYRANNOSAURUS REX

Hey Hadley, what do you call a group of singing dinosaurs? A Tyranno-chorus!

Good one, Dad! What do you call a dinosaur that's a noisy sleeper? A Tyranno-snorus!

Draw the eye, face, and front of the body. Begin the front limb.

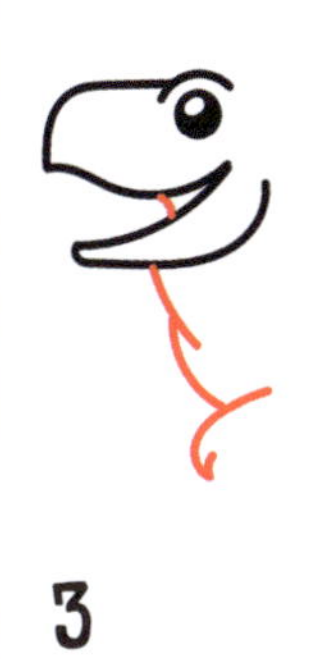

Add sharp teeth. Then follow the steps in red to build the head and body.

Develop the limbs and add a curved tail.

Add finishing touches such as skin folds and toenails.

DID YOU KNOW?

Called T. rex for short, this giant carnivore had banana-sized teeth, a relatively large brain, and small but sharp claws. It's no wonder this dinosaur's name means "tyrant lizard king"!

2

Ada the APATOSAURUS

Draw the eye and face. Then begin the long, curved neck and forelimb.

1

2

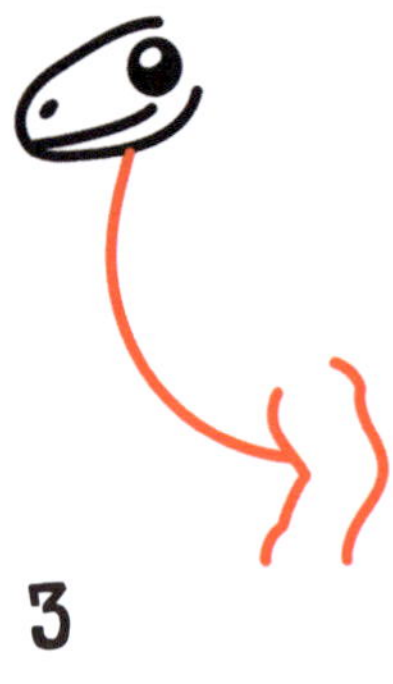

3

Develop the limbs, and add the back of the head and neck.

4

5

6

Draw the humped back and long tail. Add toenails and skin folds.

7

8

DID YOU KNOW?

The Apatosaurus lived alongside the Stegosaurus (page 26) and Allosaurus (page 42) in what is now North America. These huge herbivores had long, whip-like tails and peg-like teeth that helped them strip leaves from branches.

To give your dino depth and dimension, shade the underside of the body and head, and around the limbs.

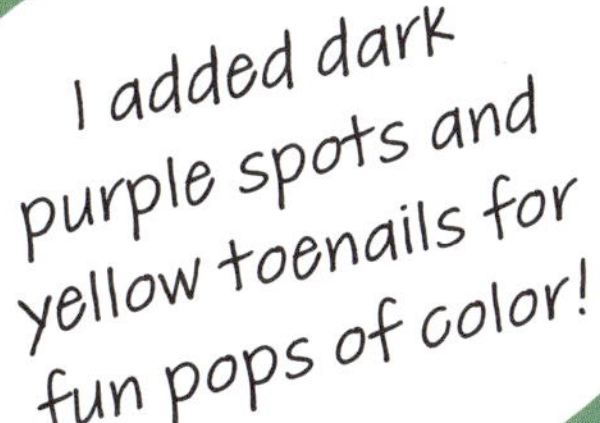

I added dark purple spots and yellow toenails for fun pops of color!

Try This!

Dress this dinosaur in roller skates, knee pads, and a helmet, and it will be ready to hit the rink!

1

Isabel the ICHTHYOSAURUS

This prehistoric reptile looked a bit like a dolphin, but it had a vertical tail like a fish.

DID YOU KNOW?

The marine-dwelling Ichthyosaurus breathed air through its nostrils, which are located at the base of its snout.

It also had a dorsal fin on its back, flippers, and a long snout. I made mine pink with yellow spots!

Try This!

Turn to pages 88–94 to learn how to make a folding surprise drawing. Then create an ocean scene that opens to reveal an Ichthyosaurus under the surface.

Start by drawing this creature's eye and snout.

1

2

Add the body, two flippers, and the dorsal fin on top.

3

4

Draw the other flippers and the scooped tail fin.

5

2

Quincy the QUETZALCOATLUS

This giant pterosaur (or flying reptile) had a fancy head crest and a pair of large wings.

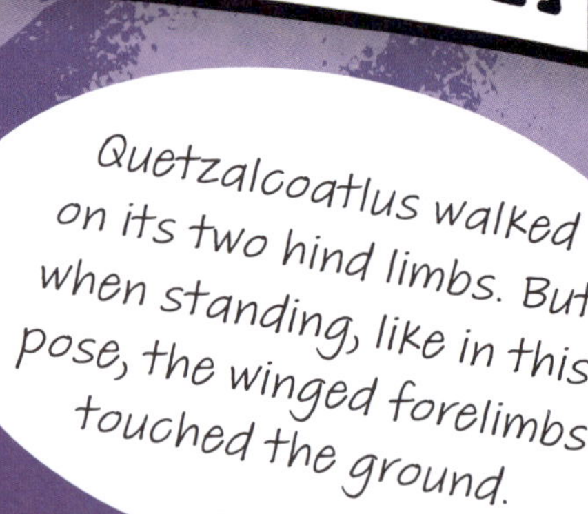

Quetzalcoatlus walked on its two hind limbs. But when standing, like in this pose, the winged forelimbs touched the ground.

Begin by drawing the eye, pointed beak, head, and neck.

1

2

3

Now add the wings, body, and limbs.

4

5

6

Follow the lines in red to finish up the last details.

7

DID YOU KNOW?

Standing as tall as a giraffe and boasting a wingspan of more than 30 feet, the Quetzalcoatlus is considered to be the largest flying animal ever to have roamed (and soared over!) the Earth.

3

Andy the ANKYLOSAURUS

This dino had bony armor-like plates on its body. It weighed about 5 to 7 tons!

My favorite feature is the round club on the end of its tail!

Draw the head and face. Start the body.

1

2

3

Add horns on the head and develop the limbs, body, and back.

4

5

6

Draw the clubbed tail, plates of armor, and spikes. Then finish the limbs.

7

8

Finish by drawing another row of spikes, toenails, and skin folds.

9

DID YOU KNOW?

The Ankylosaurus was an herbivore that ate low-to-the-ground vegetation. To protect itself from predators, it could swing its clubbed tail from side to side with great force.

2

Edward the EDMONTONIA

Start with the head, chest, and front limb.

1

2

3

Continue drawing the legs. Add the armored back and tail.

4

5

6

Now add the sharp spikes, horns, and final details.

7

8

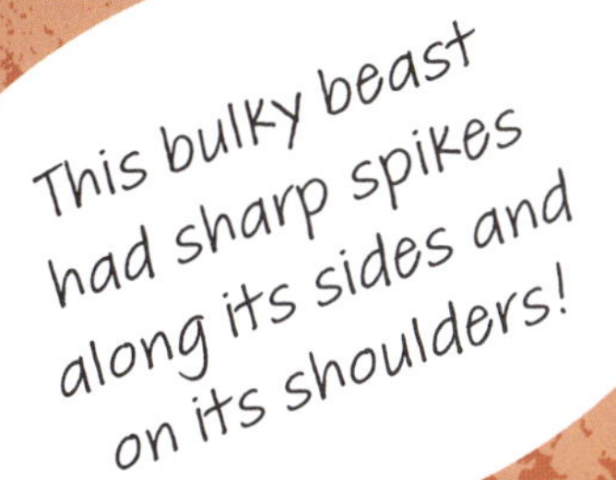

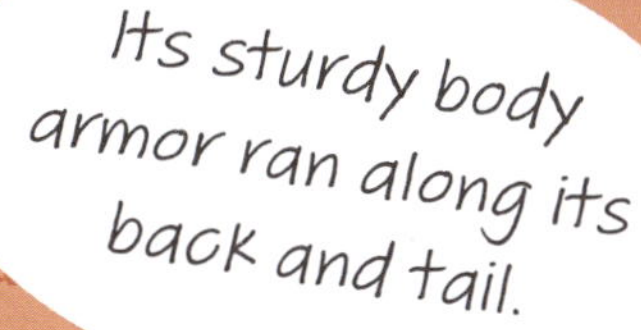

Try This!

This dinosaur was an herbivore, but that doesn't mean it wasn't a fighter! Put those spikes to use and stage an exciting battle in your drawing.

2

Nate the NOTHOSAURUS

Scientists believe this dino is distantly related to modern lizards and snakes.

Try This!

This little guy looks cute enough to be a pet! If you had a pet dinosaur, what would it look like? Draw it now!

Don't forget the chompers! It had lots of needle-like teeth on its jaw, which helped it catch slippery fish.

TRIASSIC

Draw the head, chest, and front limb. Begin drawing the sharp teeth.

1

2

Follow the lines in red to draw the back, tail, teeth, limbs, and toes.

3

4

Add stripes and webbed feet. Then add color!

5

DID YOU KNOW?

This reptile was semi-aquatic, spending its time on seashores and in shallow waters. It had webbed feet for swimming and a strong tail that helped propel it through the water.

2

Victor the VELOCIRAPTOR

Follow the lines in red to draw the eye, head, and front of the body.

1

2

3

Develop the feathered limbs and tail.

4

5

6

Follow the steps to complete the drawing.

7

8

DID YOU KNOW?

With a name that means "speedy thief," the Velociraptor was a small but swift carnivore that likely ate reptiles, eggs, and small herbivores.

Velociraptors had feathers, so I added them to the tail, arms, and back of the head.

The Velociraptor foot had three toes, but one toe on each foot pointed upward and had a long claw. Include these in your drawing!

What would this dino look like as a superhero with a cape and a mask? What superpowers would it have?

3

Dan the DACENTRURUS

DID YOU KNOW?

This large herbivore was about 30 feet long and weighed about 14,000 pounds. It had two rows of triangular plates on its back and four large tail spikes. It may have also had shoulder spikes like other stegosaur species.

Begin by drawing the head and front of the neck.

1

2

Add the back of the neck, chest, and nearest limbs. Draw a long line for the back and tail.

3

4

Draw the bottom of the tail, two shoulder spikes, triangular plates, and feet.

5

6

Add more plates, tail spikes, toenails, and skin folds. Now add color!

7

Terry the PTERODACTYL

Unlike the feathered birds of today, this flier's wings were made of skin—similar to a bat's wings.

Try This!

Draw a Pterodactyl flying over a prehistoric landscape. Add volcanoes, rivers, cliffs, and vegetation. For more ideas, see page 84.

I gave mine a crazy pattern of spots and stripes to match its weird head and body.

Draw the eye, beak, mouth, and head crest. Start the neck, body, and forelimb.

1

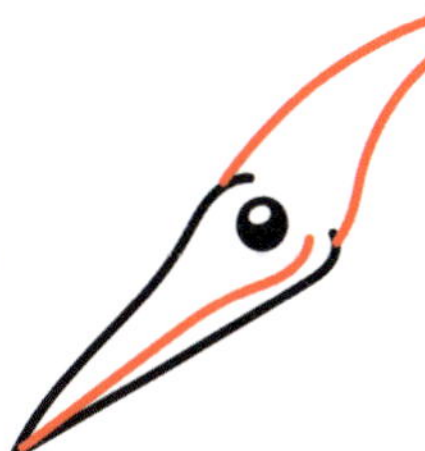

2

3

Follow the steps in red to develop the limbs.

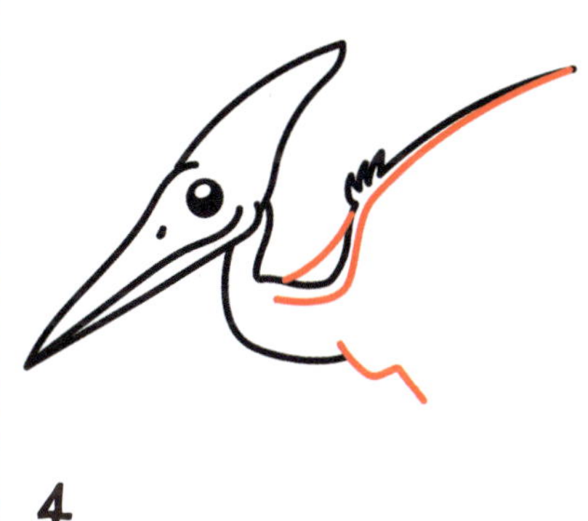

4

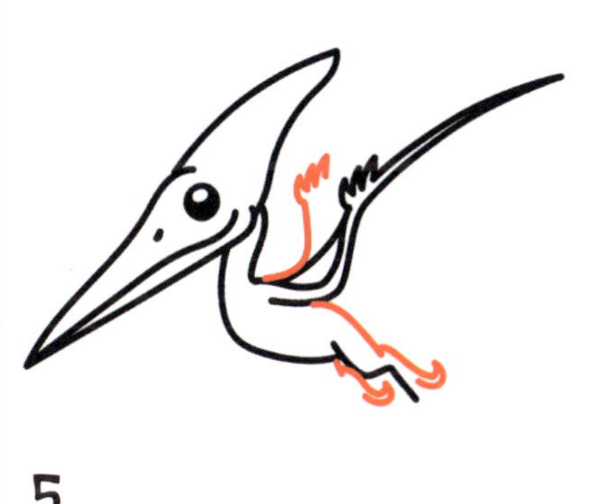

5

6

Finish the wings and feet. Now it's time to add color!

7

DID YOU KNOW?

These flying reptiles varied greatly in size. Some were the size of a sparrow; others were the size of a small airplane!

1

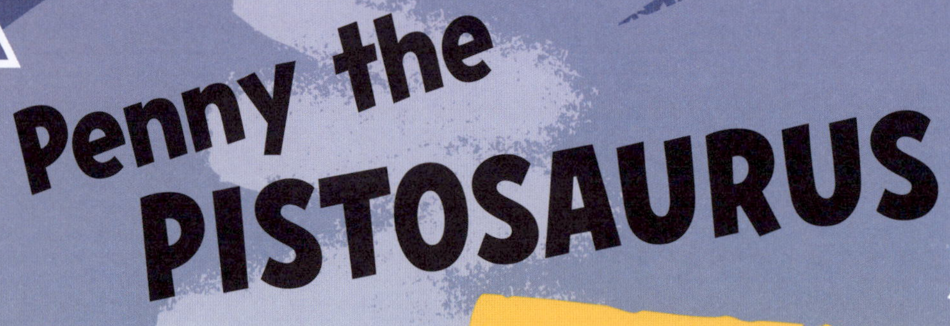

Penny the PISTOSAURUS

I love that we both chose green and yellow for our creatures, Olivia. They're twins!

Try This!

Wouldn't this dinosaur look funny in a swimsuit? Try drawing one for it now. Better yet, draw it a collection of swimwear!

They look cute. It's hard to imagine that they were 10 feet long!

Draw the head, neck, and front flipper.

1

2

Now add the other flipper, belly, tail, and back.

3

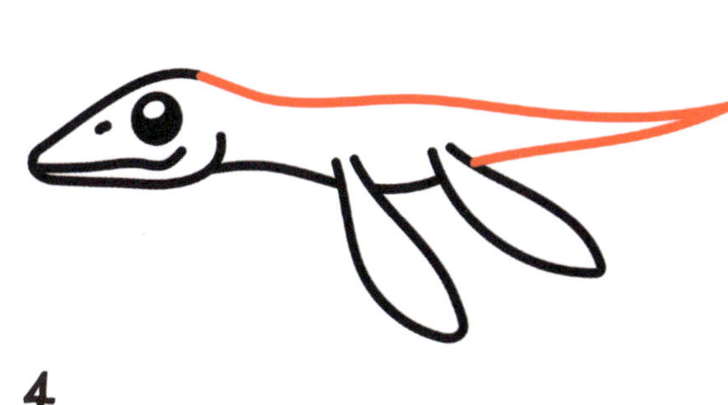

4

Draw the two far flippers, and then you're ready to add color!

5

DID YOU KNOW?

The Pistosaurus was a marine reptile discovered in what is now France and Germany. It had a body similar to the Nothosaurus (page 56) and a head similar to the Plesiosaurus (page 70).

Baxter the BAGACERATOPS

Begin with an eye, a wavy mouth, and the jaw.

1

2

Complete the head and begin building the body.

3

4

DID YOU KNOW?

With a name that means "small-horned face," the Bagaceratops had a beak-like mouth with a small horn on its snout. This dinosaur wasn't very big at all—it measured a little over 3 feet long.

Draw the back and pointed tail. Finish the limbs and final details.

5

6

I used a bunch of colors in my drawing to make a really wild dino!

I made this dinosaur darker on top and lighter on the underbelly. This coloration is called countershading, and you can see it on reptiles, fish, and lots of other animals.

Try This!

Create a wild dinosaur from your own imagination—how about a two-headed, three-tailed creature? What would you call it?

3

Alice the AMMONITE

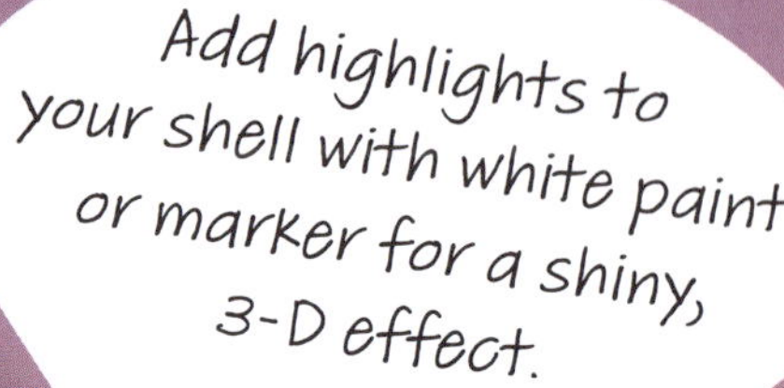

I used the complementary colors red and green. Placing them next to each other makes them appear brighter.

Draw the eye and outline of the shell.

1

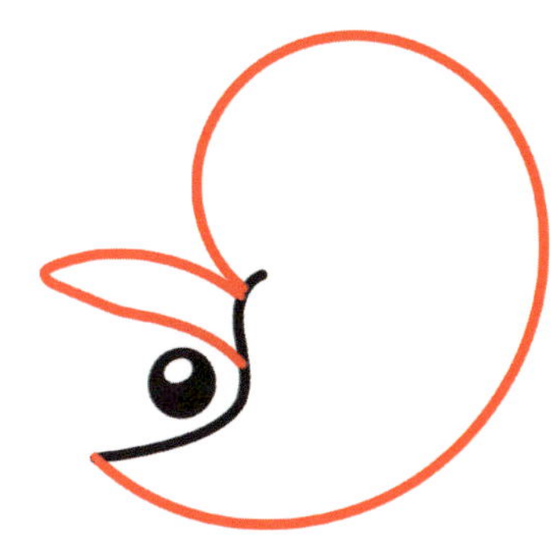

2

Add tentacles and the shell's spiral.

3

4

Complete the tentacles and draw tapered bands on the shell.

5

6

Now color your sea creature!

DID YOU KNOW?

Ammonites are most closely related to modern-day squid and octopuses. Scientists have discovered more than 10,000 different species that lived during the Jurassic and Cretaceous Periods.

Poppy the PLESIOSAURUS

Try This!

Dinos were competitive, but how would they perform as Olympic athletes? Imagine T. rex (page 44) as a boxer, Plesiosaurus as a diver, and Velociraptor (page 58) as a gymnast. Draw a scene filled with dinosaur Olympians. Who will take home the gold?

I like to think of this animal as part lizard, part dolphin!

Draw the eye, open mouth, and head.

1

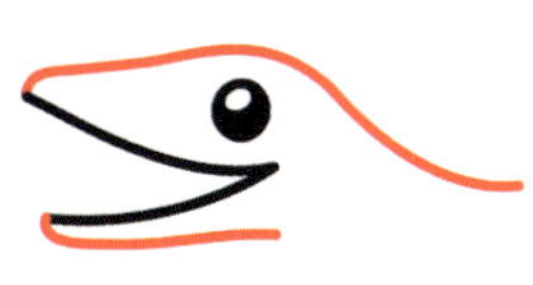

2

Add the top row of teeth, neck, two flippers, and belly.

3

4

Now draw the bottom row of teeth, tail, and remaining flippers.

5

6

Add color to finish your drawing!

DID YOU KNOW?

This long-necked marine reptile used its sharp teeth to snap up prey. In 1823, fossil-hunter Mary Anning became the first to find a nearly complete Plesiosaurus fossil in the cliffs above the English Channel.

2

Drake the DRACOREX

DID YOU KNOW?

Dracorex walked on two legs and ate plants. It lived in what is now Asia and North America.

Draw the eye, mouth, and part of the head.

1

2

Add horns to the head and draw the neck, belly, and nearest limbs.

3

4

Draw the beak, more head spikes, and develop the limbs.

5

6

CRETACEOUS

Now draw the back, tail, and other details. Then add color!
7
This dino's spiky head makes it look like a dragon. No wonder its name means "dragon king"!
After applying color, I like to outline my drawings in black marker to give them a polished look.

2

Harry the HENODUS CHELYOPS

Hey Teryn, what do you call a Henodus chelyops birthday party?

Try This!

Doesn't this ancient creature look a bit like a tortoise? Draw your favorite dinos and reptiles. Then draw their modern-day look-alikes. How are they similar? How are they different?

Oh, I know! A shell-abration!

DID YOU KNOW?

Similar to a turtle, this prehistoric animal's body was protected by a plated shell.

Draw the eye, head, and part of the shell.

1

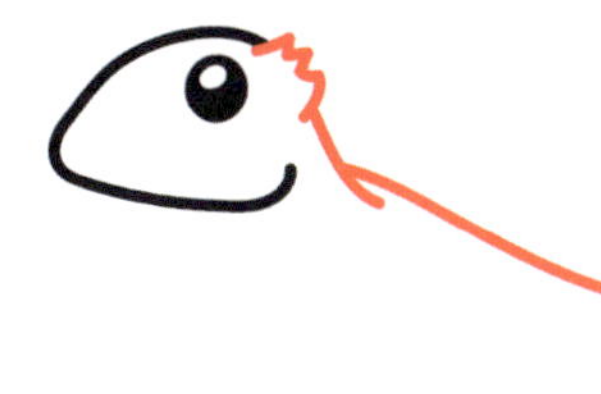

2

Finish the face. Then add the neck and the front leg.

3

4

Outline the shell and continue adding limbs.

5

6

After adding the final details, bring it to life with color!

7

2

Stan the STAURIKOSAURUS

Begin by drawing the eye and face.

1

2

3

Complete the head and start the neck, forelimb, and hind leg.

4

5

6

Draw the back and tail, and continue adding to the limbs.

7

8

9

DID YOU KNOW?
Discovered in what is now Brazil, this small dinosaur was a speedy carnivore that lived during the Late Triassic Period. It stretched about 7 feet long and walked on its hind legs.
Now finish the front claws and feet.
10
I gave my dino light stripes, gray claws, and a white underbelly.
I colored mine pink and then added zigzags to the skin using thin, purple lines.

Part II: YOU'RE AN ARTIST!

In this section, you'll learn how to draw things that add interest to your art. I've also included instructions for creating two folding surprise drawings. Remember, there are no mistakes—your only goal is to have fun!

Expressions

In cartoon drawing, expressions are often used to give characters personality. Experiment giving your dinosaurs (and other things) emotions through happy, angry, or scared facial expressions. Try other expressions, if you like.

HAPPY

Use bright eyes and a wide smile for a happy face.

ANGRY

Use narrowed eyebrows and a large, squared open mouth to display anger.

SCARED

Draw upturned eyebrows and a downturned mouth to express fear.

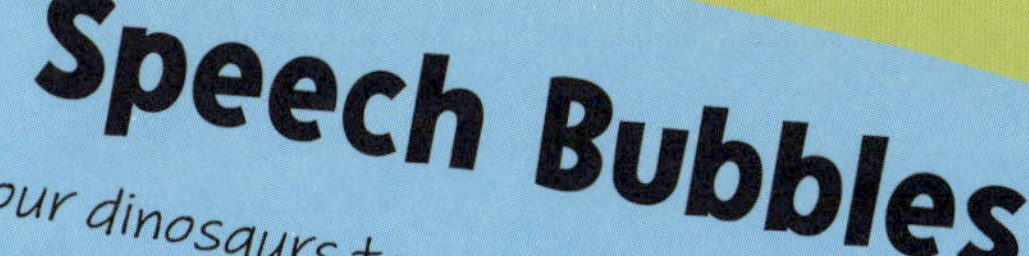

Speech Bubbles

Allow your dinosaurs to communicate or express thoughts through speech bubbles.

Round and rectangular speech bubbles give your characters the ability to "talk" to each other or your readers.

This speech bubble is used to express enthusiasm or excitement!

This thought cloud reveals a character's internal thoughts to the reader.

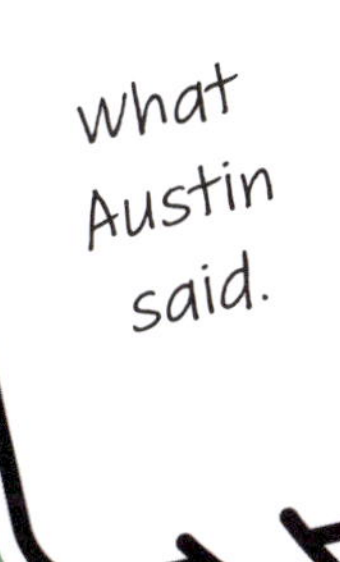

Action & Movement

These fun details can add interest to your dinosaur drawings by showing them in action and bringing them to life.

ROARING

Draw lightning bolts to illustrate sound coming from the mouth.

RUNNING

Use parallel lines behind a dinosaur to show speed.

STOMPING

Draw a lifted leg, action lines, and poofs of dust to suggest a heavy stomp.

HATCHING

Draw cracks and pieces of shell for a hatching egg.

CHOMPING

Draw a burst to show the dinosaur chomping away with its sharp teeth.

SWISHING

Use dashed, curving lines to show a tail swishing through the air.

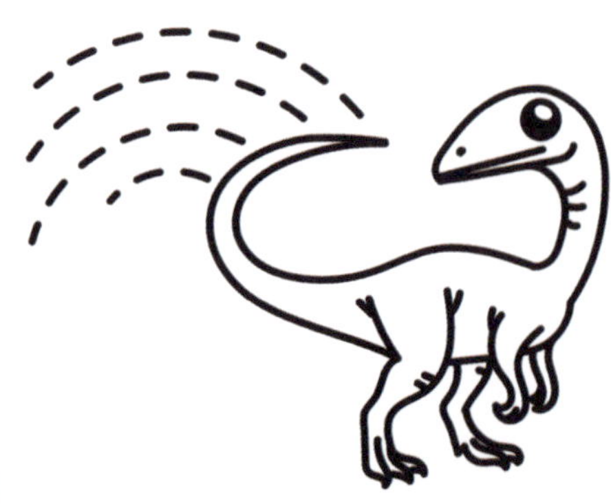

Prehistoric PROPS

Props are objects that add character, style, and a sense of place to your drawings. Insects and critters are great additions to prehistoric scenes!

Beetle

Start with a U shape for the body and wings. Follow the steps in red to complete the beetle.

Lizard

Draw the eye and head, followed by a long line for the back and tail. Then develop the limbs.

Dragonfly

Begin with a head with large eyes and a round body. Then add wings and a long tail.

I love imagining what it's like to be a paleontologist digging for bones. In addition to the props I've drawn, what other prehistoric treasures can you think up to draw?

Bone

Draw a set of parallel lines. Then add the rounded end of each bone.

Vertebrae

Outline the length of the spine. Add short lines to show the vertebrae (or backbones). Then draw thin rib-like bones along the spine.

Dino Skull

Begin with the top and front of the skull. Draw a hole for the eye and sharp teeth. Add the lower jaw, nasal cavity, and a few more details.

Trilobite Fossil

This prehistoric marine animal existed long before the dinosaurs. Start with an oval and follow the steps in red to draw this fossil.

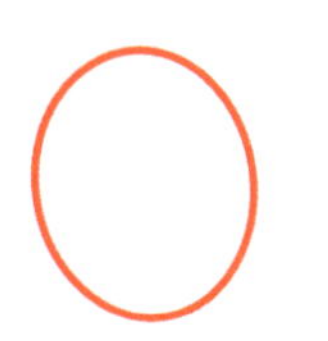
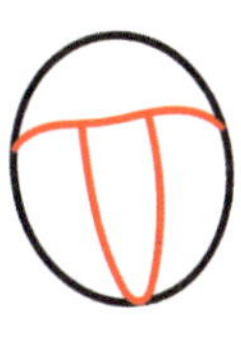

Dino Skeleton

Begin with the head and spine. Add short lines for the vertebrae, sharp teeth, and plates along the back. Finish with thin rib bones.

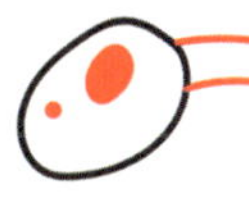
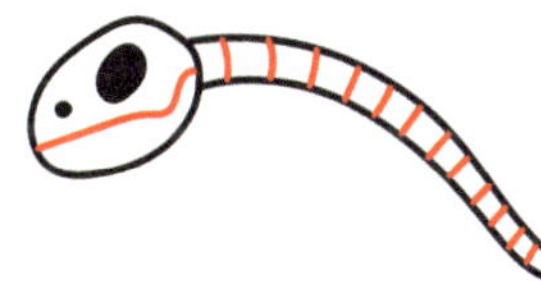

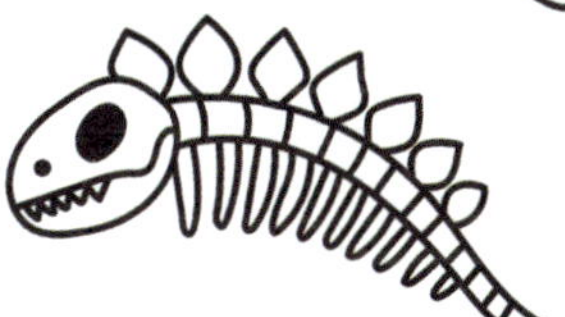

Footprint Fossil

Draw an irregular shape for the stone. Then outline the dinosaur's footprint, including the sharp claws. Add a few pebble-like shapes to finish.

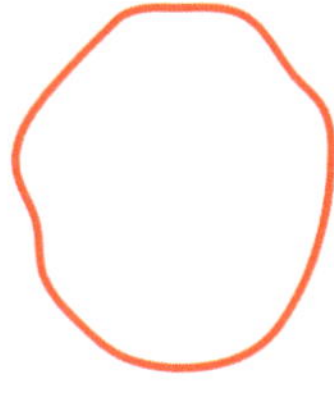
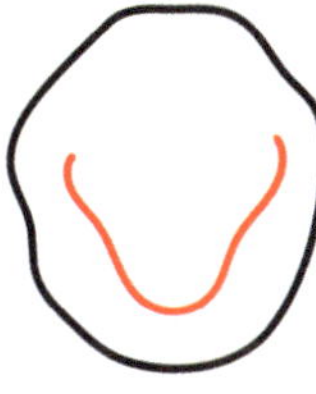
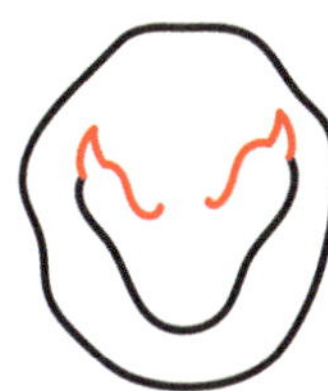

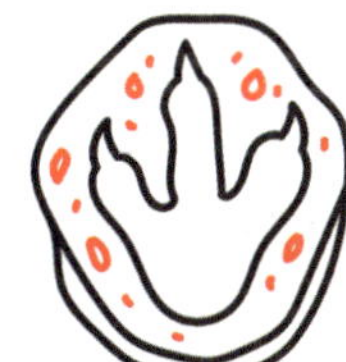
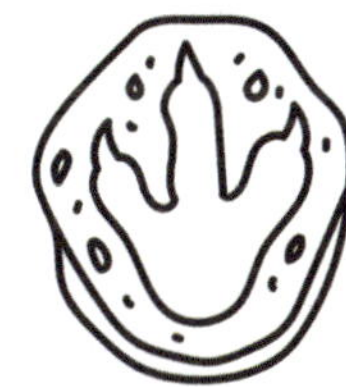

Fern

Draw a small mound of dirt and a curl for each stem. Develop the leaves with scalloped edges for a fluffy, feather-like appearance.

Volcano

Begin with the base of the volcano. Add the mountain, crater, lava, and some clouds of gas.

Bubbling Bog

Wet environments like bogs and swamps were common when the dinosaurs lived. Begin with an irregular oval. Then add bubbles on and above the surface. Draw little bursts to show bubbles popping.

Mossy Log

Begin with an oval and a spiral for the end of the log. Create a cylinder and add clumps of moss.

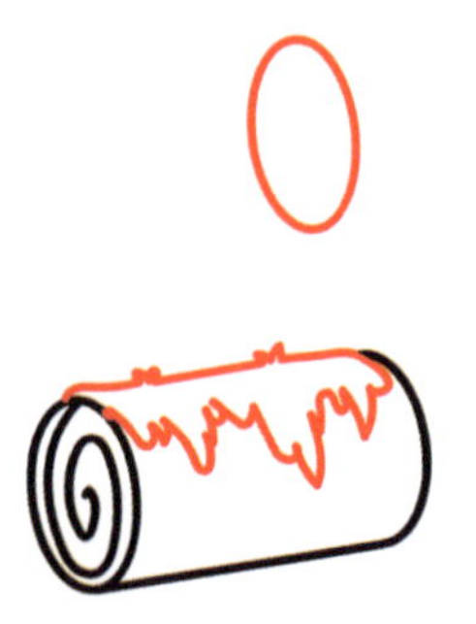

Prehistoric Trees

For each tree, start with the trunk and then add foliage. Finish with details, such as thorns or grass.

Cycad

Start with a line for the ground and two lines for the sides of the wide trunk. Add lots of pointed leaves, and use x marks for the trunk's texture.

Putting It ALL TOGETHER

Look how you can pull all the individual pieces together to form completed scenes. What other scenes would you like to draw?

Dinosaur Gathering

Excavation Site

Below are some more tool ideas for adding to your dig scene! Draw a trowel, brush, magnifying glass, mallet, and chisel.

Folding SURPRISE DRAWINGS

A folding surprise drawing is exactly what it sounds like: a drawing on folded paper that opens to reveal a surprise inside! This project is a lot of fun and gives you an opportunity to stretch your creativity.

Before you begin, you'll need to prepare your paper so the surprise works the way it should. I used a sheet of printer paper (8.5 x 11 inches), but you can use any size paper you like.

Paper Set Up

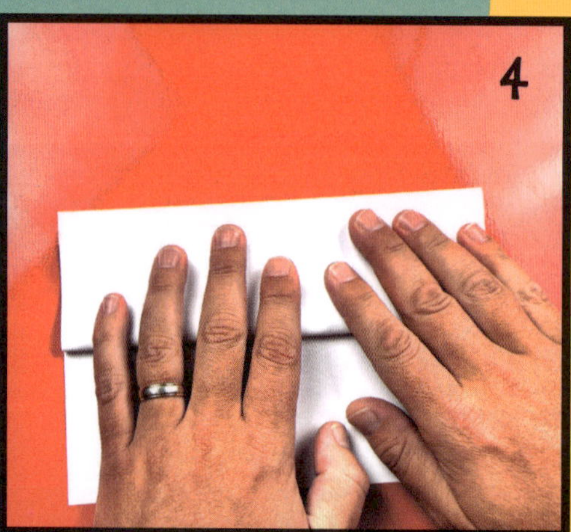

1. Lay the paper flat with the short sides of the paper on the top and bottom, and the long sides of the paper on the left and right. Fold the paper in half, lining up the top edge with the bottom edge.

2. Press along the fold to make a crease.

3. Gently lift the top flap of the paper.

4. Fold the top flap up, bringing the bottom edge to line up with the top edge. Press along the fold to make another crease.

5. and 6. Lift the paper and flip it over from right to left, so that the unfolded bottom flap is now on the top.

7. Lift the flap and fold it up to meet the top edge, repeating step 4.

8. Open the last fold you just made.

9. Flip your paper over from left to right, so it's back to the original side.

10. Your paper is now ready for your drawing! You will start the outside drawing on the folded paper.

Note: When you unfold the page, you should have four sections marked by folds.

Turn the page to get started on the first surprise drawing!

Folding DINOSAUR CHOMP

FOLDED

1. Place the paper with the folded side up (see step 10 on page 89). Draw the top of the head.

2. Now add the eye and the nostril. Draw the bottom of the jaw and the back of the neck, connecting the lines along the fold.

3. Trace along the fold to add the mouth. Draw the front of the neck, and add zigzags for the spikes along the top of the head.

4. Continue the zigzags down the back of the neck. Finish by adding a few stripes across the front of the neck.

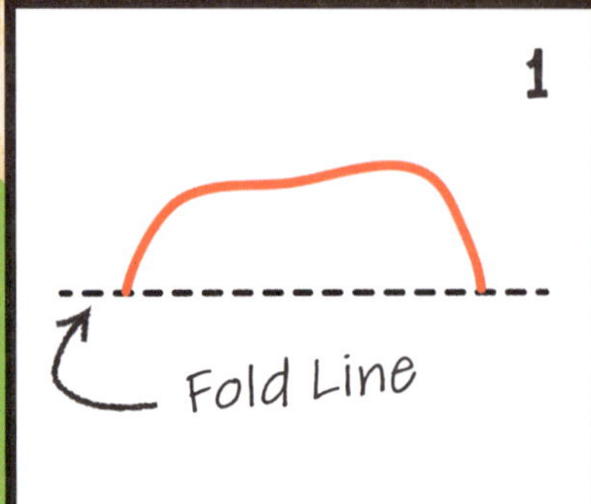

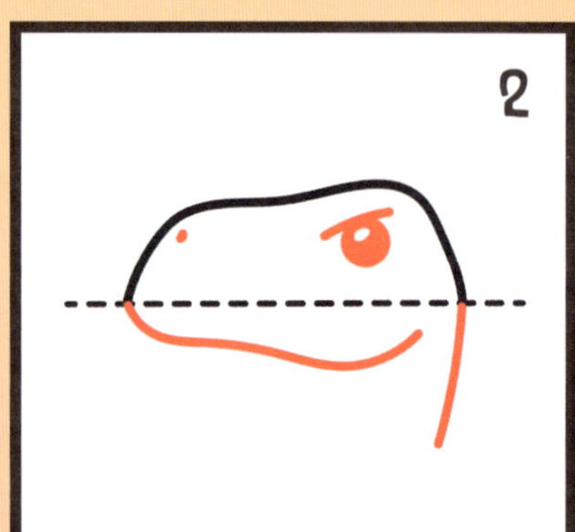

Turn the page to see how I colored this dino head.

OPENED

1. Unfold your paper. Then draw a line connecting the sides of the mouth and a line connecting the back of the head.
2. Add two rows of sharp teeth and a pointed tongue.
3. Draw the far side of the mouth. Begin the bones with some parallel lines.
4. Then finish the bones, throat, and spikes down the back of the head.

COLOR YOUR DRAWING

1

1. Refold the paper so only the outside drawing is visible. Then add color with the art tools of your choice.

2

2. Open the paper and color the inside of the mouth. I used pink for the tongue, red for the throat, and blue shadows for the teeth and bones.

1

Hatching DINOSAUR EGG

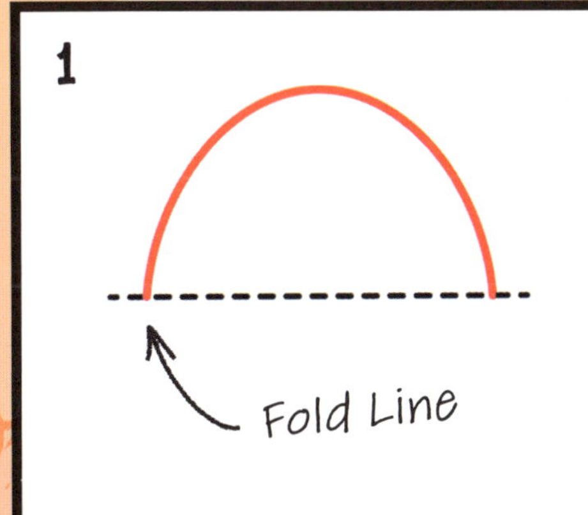

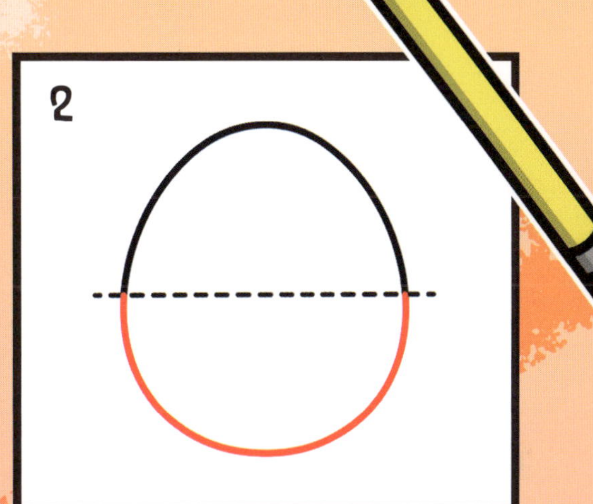

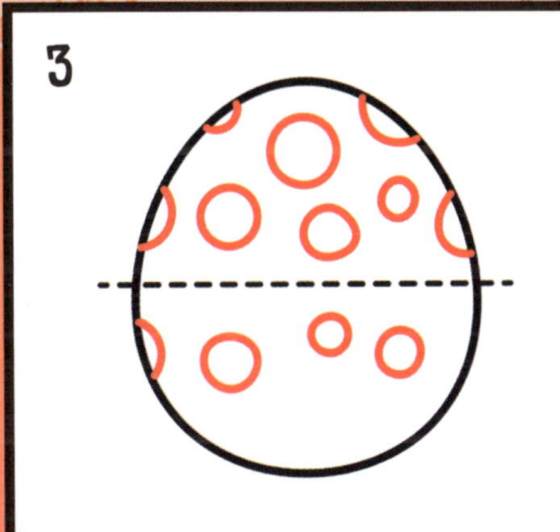

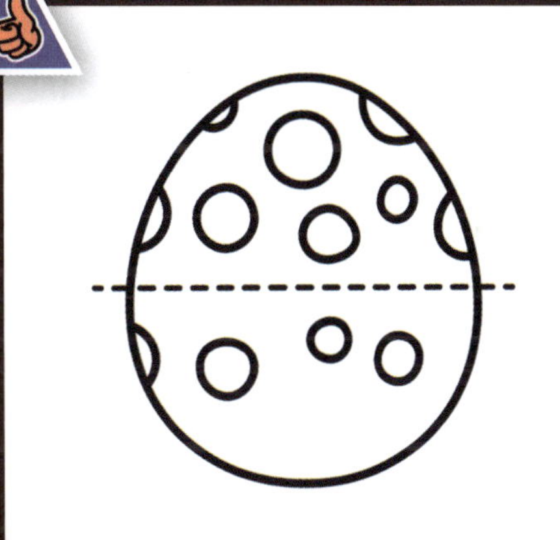

FOLDED

1. Place the paper with the folded side up (see step 10 on page 89). Draw the top of the egg with an arched line.

2. Then draw the lower half of the egg, connecting the line to both sides of the top half.

3. Add spots and speckles to the egg's shell.

OPENED

1.–3. Unfold your paper so the egg is split. Begin drawing the edges of the broken shell, front legs, and top of the head.

4.–5. Add the eye, nostril, mouth, and pointed tail.

6.–7. Draw two rows of sharp teeth and spikes along the head, back, and tail. Add a few stripes across the underbelly. Finish by drawing bits of egg shell.

Don't forget to color in your drawing. What will you name this new baby dino?

1

Top Fold

Bottom Fold

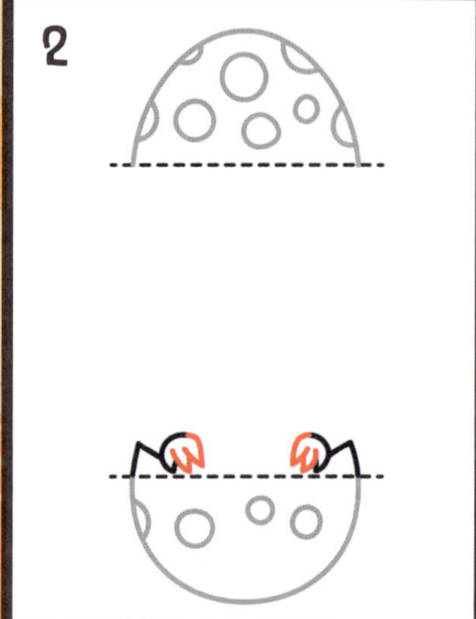

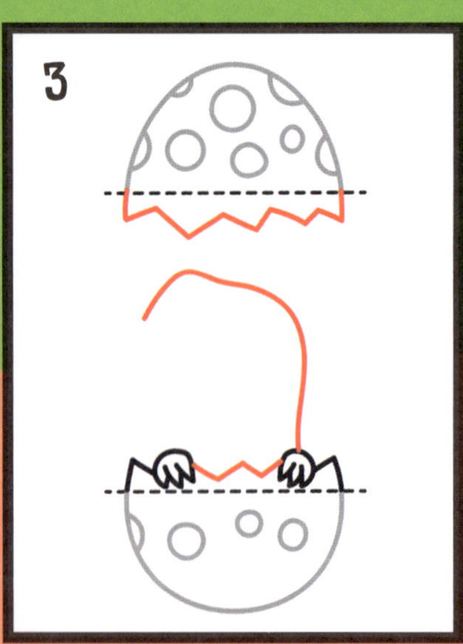

ABOUT THE ARTIST

Rob Jensen, the fun-loving creator of Art for Kids Hub, has a background in industrial design, which fuels his passion for teaching art. He believes that creativity adds happiness and interest to life. Rob, along with his family, embodies the spirit of making art both easy and exciting. Collectively, the Jensens demonstrate that art is not just a solo journey but a shared family adventure. Together, they show the world how to create art in simple, engaging ways, one drawing at a time.

ABOUT ART FOR KIDS HUB

Art for Kids Hub is a family-driven platform that brings the joy of art to families around the world. Co-created by Rob Jensen and his family, it offers a friendly, welcoming space for kids of all ages to learn and grow artistically. Recognized by various media outlets, Art for Kids Hub provides a diverse range of resources, including an engaging website, an online shop, and social media content full of art lessons. This platform is committed to making learning art fun and accessible, showcasing that art can be a delightful experience for everyone. It complements traditional art teaching by adding its unique, family-oriented touch. Visit artforkidshub.com.

SOME WORDS OF GRATITUDE

In the creation of this book, I've been surrounded by an incredible circle of support and inspiration, each person contributing uniquely to this journey.

To Teryn, my wife and partner in everything: Your love, support, and friendship are the cornerstones of not only this book but of all our endeavors. I am endlessly grateful for your presence in my life. You make everything possible.

My deepest gratitude also goes to our children—Jack, Hadley, Austin, and Olivia. Your creativity, laughter, and shared joy in art have been the foundation of not only this book but all we do at Art for Kids Hub. You are my heart and inspiration.

A heartfelt thank you to DK, my publisher, for believing in this project. Pete Jorgensen, who first reached out to me with this wonderful opportunity: Your confidence in my work has been a great honor. Working with DK has been an enriching and fulfilling experience.

Special appreciation goes to Rebecca Razo and Elizabeth Gilbert at Coffee Cup Creative, LLC. Your expertise and vision have been instrumental in bringing this book to life. Your dedication and skill have transformed my ideas into something tangible and beautiful.

To my parents, Greg and Ruth Jensen, thank you for your unwavering encouragement and support since my childhood. Your belief in my passion for drawing has been a guiding light throughout my life and career.

I am also profoundly grateful to the young artists and their families who have joined us on Art for Kids Hub. Your enthusiasm and creativity have been a continuous source of inspiration and joy.

To the broader community of educators, fellow artists, and supporters, thank you for your encouragement and invaluable feedback. You have helped foster a nurturing space for young artists to thrive.

This book is a tribute to all of you. Your support, in so many ways, has made this journey an enriching and joyous adventure. Thank you for being part of our art family!

Rob Jensen